Thick Black Lines

poems by

Christie Cruise

Finishing Line Press
Georgetown, Kentucky

Thick Black Lines

Dedicated to the memories of
Geraldine (mama), Donta, and Danielle

ACKNOWLEDGMENTS

Other, *Remington Review*, Fall 2020
This, Is America, *Our Stories, Ourselves: Narratives of Black Women in Africa
and America*, April 2021
Black Girl Magic, *Heels into the Soil: Stories and Poems Resisting the Silence*,
2021
Interrogation of Justice (previous iteration, Interrogation of Injustice), *Heels
into the Soil: Stories and Poems Resisting the Silence*, 2021
The Bough, *Kitchen Table Quarterly*, Winter 2021
The Uncaged Bird, *Black Minds Mag*, March 2022

Publisher: Leah Huete de Maines
Editor: Christen Kincaid
Cover Art: Katie Wright, Katie Wright Photography
Author Photo: Katie Wright, Katie Wright Photography
Cover Design: Elizabeth Maines McCleavy

Order online: www.finishinglinepress.com
also available on amazon.com

Author inquiries and mail orders:
Finishing Line Press
PO Box 1626
Georgetown, Kentucky 40324
USA

Contents

THICK

/THik/
Deep or dense, heavy

The Bough

I break open.
Each time I remember to whom I am born,
I break open.
Like a pumpkin cradled in the arms
of a clumsy child careening to the ground,
I break open.
Like fresh brown ones and white ones
clacked on the rim of a cold ceramic bowl,
I break open.
When lips part to share the secret
that no other soul can know,
I break
open.

The Day My Mother Died

It was a Monday.
It was the eighth day in the fourth month
of that year. That's the day my soul broke
open. As a result, I shattered
into fragments of flesh and shards
of bone. My soul evaporated
on that day and I watched
through sockets encircled with soggy lashes.
And each day after, a centripetal force
has whisked the remaining particles
together to form something—
a shell of my former self—something
blue and gray and absent of the contents
that matter most. Mondays
in the fourth month are unlike
Mondays in the three months before and eight after.
Then again, I don't expect them to feel
as they did before my soul consumed
the axe that broke it open to begin with.

Reluctance

I.
I awoke to myself. Once.
It was startling to see me
lying there as if nothing
could touch the space where love
and longing lie. Once,
I awoke to myself. It was that time
where love and longing might
have touched if they weren't lying
on either side of hurt. As if nothing
could heal me, I decided to lie
there. I was startled by my own
assumptions about love and longing.
I touched the space within myself. Once.
It was light as air.

II.
I scoured the earth in search of something,
anything that could make me feel
whole. But there was nothing.
There was no one.
I closed my eyes,
imagined the sunrise within,
and held space for me.
I offered to myself the gift
of being present, to embrace
who I am, and to explore
my emotions, intimately.
Then, I found myself. I spoke
truth. It poured from my lips like
fresh water from a spring.
I am whole. Again.

Depression Be Like

Today was a good day.
I showered. Warm water cleansed
the space between my thighs
and she rejoiced like the desert
when it rains.

Today was a good day.
I shaved. The razor glided
across parts that already resemble
a feline Sphynx. It was just the act
of it that was satisfying.

Moussed fingers ran through
two-month-old crochet braids.
I laid my edges down gentle
like spreading icing on a cake.

Mother of pearl teeth felt
the brush scrub in circular motions
then up and down preceded
by a string of mint between them.

Mucous encrusted eyes doused
with water for the first time
in over 48 hours, opened to observe
the ruins of the rest of me.

Today was a good day.
I made my way to the couch.
Then, to the patio doors.
There was no breeze, but
the air was fresh.

Today was a good day.
I watched the birds play
by the key lime tree.
I envied their wings. I
wanted to fly away.

Freshly moisturized feet trekked
back to the bedroom.
The air was stale. I opened
a window. Perhaps tomorrow
I'll wash the sheets.

Insomnia Haikus

I.
You died and I did
not cry. In the dirt, I will
plant lilies, daisies.

II.
Impermanence—You,
cherry blossoms, butterflies.
I needed more time.

III.
Bury me with her.
I cannot breathe above ground.
Grief has strangled me.

IV.
I listen to the
rain fall outside my window
and I can stand it.

V.
I want to show you
what I carry. I want to
show you why I dream.

VI.
Breaking through twilight
like a crowning baby. Make
your entrance, sunrise.

The Uncaged Bird

Sing, bird. Sing loud and strong.
Let your song echo throughout the earth.
Let the waters swell from the vibrations
of your breath. Powerful. Proud. Bravado.
I hear your song, the melody you carry,
often alone. You will always have
an audience with me, ears listening
attentively, waiting for your next run
and riff. I recognize many of those songs,
demands for justice, to be seen, acknowledged.
But you have wings. Fly away free.

Haiku for My Left Breast

Benign breast lesion.
A beautiful incision.
Pus seething beneath.

While You Were Judging Me for Being Fat

I was carrying weight a scale could never measure.
I was creating, for my body, a cloak of protection, a cocoon to render
me invisible. I hid in leaves of chocolates and potato chips
from the calls of boys and men with ill intentions. This was no
garden and the tree of knowledge bore fruit from which no child
should be offered to eat.

I was considering ways in which to end my suffering.
I was debating, in a last act of kindness, the most humane way to
cease to exist. I cut the stem of a flower with a steak knife,
the serrated edges ripping away flesh during the dress rehearsal.
There was to be no opening night. Children shouldn't play with dead
things.

I was emptying the contents of a knapsack filled with insecurities.
I was releasing no's and maybe's and reclaiming dreams deferred and
hopes delayed. I embraced faults and flaws, removing doubts
about not being enough and being too much. The more I unpacked
the lighter I became, rising above droughts and dry lands of bones,
desert clay, and sand.

I was becoming the woman I saw in my dreams.
I was envisioning my body free from the chains of myths and
stereotypes about its size and color.
I loved the idea of no longer succumbing
to the expectations of those who knew nothing of me as soft and
human. That premium space now occupied by adoration from the
one whose opinions matter most.

I was finding my voice, hanging on its every word.
I was exploring my being—body, mind, and spirit.
I found a sacred place within me—fat, Black, beautiful me.
And, oh, the heavens I hold, inconceivable to the nonbeliever.
And, oh, the heavens I hold.

#ThemToo

When families and communities cover a predator through silence,
the broken hymens he leaves in his wake are untold.
She's a fast ass. She knew better.
That's what they said about the pregnant 12-year-old.
No *Roe v. Wade* protections then or now.
That's what they said about Aaliyah.
His music catalog too clutch to acknowledge his crimes.

Then there was us.
Those of us who were silenced
Because maybe, just maybe we were fast asses.
Maybe, just maybe, we did know better.
I am sorry. I have always wanted to say that.
I am sorry that happened to you, to us.

I am sorry
your family shamed you and labeled trauma as promiscuity.
I am sorry
you were forced to be in the presence of your perpetrator
at church and family functions and neighborhood gatherings.
I am sorry
you were not believed when you reported the assault to a trusted
adult.
I am sorry
your trusted adult wanted to please her man more than she wanted
to believe you.
I am sorry
it was easier for people to believe your "nervous breakdown" was
because you were slipped a Mickey.
I am sorry
no one has ever said to you, "I'm sorry that happened to you. It is not
your fault."
I am sorry you had to carry the burden of secrecy in your chest until
you felt safe, after his death.
I am sorry
I am only now writing this poem.

Lessons from Trees

Every year the trees strip down
and bare their souls. And, not
just for a moment. They stand there
in all their nakedness for a season—
the one where they need the covering
the most—and show us the power
and strength in vulnerability. They stand tall
and brave, never folding. And then, when
it is time, they adorn themselves
with leaves and fragrant flowers. They show
us gratitude. Having survived the coldest
season of their existence, they show us
resilience. They show us love.

BLACK

/Blak/
Relating to Black people, Black culture

Black Girl Magic

I am afraid for little Black girls.
Little Black girls have it
hard. They are not safe.
They are expected to be everything,
except little girls. Little Black girls are expected to perform
magic. What else could explain society's belief
of emotional strength and resilience in the face of constant
adversity? It would be nothing short of a magic trick
if little Black girls came through the sufferings of their
childhoods, of this life, unscathed. Yes, they are magic.
They create the illusion of well-being
when, in fact, it is absent. How can they
maintain a sense of well-being in a society
that wants to perform magic, too?
A society that wants them to disappear.
Abracadabra! Pull the curtain back. No secret
door or drop-down compartment. Little Black girls
are responsible for their own safety.
They are expected to safely navigate
the family child molester and neighborhood pedophile.
I worry about little Black girls when they are unable
to successfully traverse the landmines of sexual predators,
of poverty, and of adults with grown-up expectations.
I am afraid for little Black girls who carry trauma
inflicted on them from every corner of society.
I am afraid for them when they attend school,
and their pain manifests as bad behavior. I worry
about little Black girls, in the absence of safety
and comfort, despite the evidence of abuse
so easily spotted in other little girls, ignored
when it presents in them. Surely someone
will take notice and understand. Other
little girls receive a grace little Black girls
know nothing of, the color of their skin
has erased their innocence. Their trauma ignored
because little Black girls are sassy and bossy,

even when they are 7 years old. After all,
that's how Black women behave.
Little Black girls are adultified and dehumanized.
And, when they become women, the neglect
and disrespect continues. We need only say their names
to know how it ends for little Black girls:
Breonna Taylor, Sandra Bland, Atatiana Jefferson.
They were once little Black girls too.

Other

It was a Tuesday.
The first time I realized
I would never really be accepted,
that this society only wanted my Black body
for labor, exploitation, appropriation.
On that Tuesday, my Black voice was silenced,
the tears of a white woman pushed my Black experience to the margin
until I was invisible.

At work I listened to white women share how a new book had
empowered them to lean in.
It was a Thursday.
I remember thinking I would need to be a contortionist
to lean in from the margin,
leaning into a table to which I was never invited.

It was a Sunday.
The first time I was told by people who look like me
that I was not enough.
On that Sunday, I came to know the psychological devastation of racism,
its manifestation as internalized oppression and colorism.
I was too dark to matter.

In class the professor referred to others.
It was a Wednesday.
As he continued to lecture, I realized I was who he meant,
I was the other.
Nameless, faceless, nothingness.
I was alien, different, marginal.
I sat in that space,
present, yet absent.

It was a Saturday.
The first time I rested in the beauty of my Black womanhood,
when I spoke my truth boldly.
On that Saturday, I came to understand my power,
in whose image I was created.
I fashioned my own table, invited my sisters,
and we loved one another fiercely.

This, Is America

The immigrant yells, "Go back where you came from!"
The descendant of enslaved people responds, "Where I came from?"
I came from the womb of a Black woman,
A sacred, hallowed space
with power and energy vibrating
on a level parallel to the creator,
fashioned as the carrier of endless possibilities.
I came from the Garden of Eden
naked, natural, created in His image, the first woman.
I came from the heavens,
the firmament swathed in stars, planets, and the moon.
I came from love songs, soulful,
with melodies and chords and strings on lutes.
I came from the elements—fire, wind, water, earth, space, and time,
explosive as volcanic eruptions, overpowering as tsunamis,
entwined to the universe like the moon to the tides.
"Go back where I came from?
I AM where I came from."

Interrogation of Justice

I do not make it a habit of questioning folks about the validity
of their disability, but lady, I believe you can see. Witnesses
have said you peer from underneath the blindfold. That could explain
your depraved indifference.

For whom do you see, Themis? Which lives matter, Justitia?
Who is worthy to live, move, and have their being?
You must have seen that man keep his knee
in the neck of another, with such ease, bearing
down on flesh in the way a child presses their foot on a hose.
Wondering what will happen to water when it has no place to go.
You do know what happens when a knee crushes a trachea,
don't you? Sure, you do. A neck is not a water hose.

Please explain how playing video games, sleeping peacefully in bed,
or watching television while eating ice cream at home warrants
murder. How is stalking a child walking home with iced tea and
Skittles standing your ground? I can only imagine that you have lost
a piece of your soul. I can only imagine to whom you pray, standing
there with covered eyes, libra in one hand, sword in the other
while children sleep in feces and urine-filled cages separated from
their parents. How do you stand so proud with the knowledge that a
city has been left with sewage water for drinking and bathing?

Help me understand, Lady Justice, how voting for a candidate who
advocates grabbing women by the vagina is more acceptable than
voting, instead, for the candidate who has one? Indeed, you can see.
You have always seen. De jure, de facto oppression and segregation,
this is your legacy. This is your nation.

Attacking Critical Race Theory Won't Make Me Forget

My Black is beautiful! It is artful and poetic. It is Sugar Shack and Warrior. It is Maya and Audre. It is Zora and Toni.

My Black is the firmament! It is the canvas from which the stars hang. It is vast and engulfing. It is nothing and everything.

My Black is Black! So black it's blue-black. I wish an MF would, Black. Black sorrow, Black tears, Black blood, Black.

My Black is bold! It is unapologetic. It is fearless, it rages on. It is resilient! It never gives up. It never fails. It is love.

My Black is encompassing! It is a black hole—strong pull, stronghold. It is the moon and the tides. It is the end and the beginning.

My Black is the mother of humanity! It is Eve and Henrietta. It is Anarcha, Lucy, and Betsey. It is the cause and the cure. It is living and dying.

My Black is coveted! It is copied, reproduced, and mimicked. It is a trendsetter. It leads, guides, and is followed like the North Star.

My Black is music! It is blues and jazz. It is Coltrane and Davis. It is Blue in Green. It is an Electric Relaxation and a peaceful retreat.

My Black is spiritual! It is mountain-high and valley low. It is the Red Sea in front and the enemy behind. It has faith, it believes.

When Karens Cry

It sounds like thunder from clouds filled with the rain that will water
the seeds in the soil where trees that bear strange fruit grow.

It feels like the break of a vaginal hymen leading to rivers
flowing blood on cotton folds and sheets.

It smells like burned flesh underneath crucifixes ablaze to purify
their race; her tears the accelerant.

It tastes like calcium-filled pulp and enamel swallowed
upon the entering of a barrel in the mouth of lips pursed to whistle
songs of swing low sweet chariot.

It looks like policing Black bodies while birdwatching, barbecuing
in the park and talking on cell phones in hotel lobbies.

Karen's tears can drown a community and set it afire simultaneously.
And she won't stop.

Wherever there are Black bodies her crying commences
like a baby whose mother is no longer in view.

She is only soothed when Black bodies are subdued and put in their
place. Beneath her, below her, between a rock and a hard one. That
position familiar to Emmett Till's uncle, that space where only Black
bodies seem to fill.

Cry if you will, Karen. Your tears are a tool of the master. If you
desire shelter in the master's house, in his house is where you can
witness, through the window of distraction, our liberation.

Things Fall Apart

The night I fell through the stairs was during the pandemic.
I laughed because I thought I was dreaming.
You know the dream where you're falling and wake up
right before you splat? This was real, though. It was like
when those geese attacked me, and I pissed myself.
The night I fell through the stairs during the pandemic
I didn't piss myself. I was wet because it was raining.
I couldn't get out of the damn hole, just like I couldn't
get off the ground when the geese attacked me. The geese
were nesting. The stairs were not. They just decided
not to support me.

Those stairs must have known Don Lemon. He dropped Ma'Khia
Bryant. I guess she was too heavy. He could not withstand the weight
of her Black body. Those stairs must have known Daniel Cameron.
He dropped Breonna Taylor. She was more than he could carry.
Ma'Khia. Breonna. They were just too damn heavy.
We are all too damn heavy.

The day I fell through the stairs during the pandemic, I suppose
I laughed because I thought I was dreaming. Until I was dangling
there, screaming for help. How many times have we screamed
for help only to have our cries fall on deaf ears?
I know of at least three.

Paintings of Trees Remind Me of That Billie Holiday Song

Inspired by Paul Morrison's Cambium (El cambium)

Felled trees like Black corses
Torn bark saturated
with sap and blood. Vessels
of God, epithelial and cambium coalesced
into swaddling clothes.
I fall to my knees in prayer
and reverence. The dove
and the raven fly overhead
to comfort and remind.

LINES

/Līn/s
An agreed-upon approach; a policy

Bodies That Know Boxes

Black bodies. They know.
They know the immorality of confinement.
Black bodies know dehumanization and subjugation
for the sake of colonization.
If the body keeps the score,
Black bodies have tracked hashtags and lashes that rip
the flesh from the bone.

Black bodies. They know.
They know the trauma of subtraction.
Black bodies know separation and the tearing
apart of families. They know being forced to multiply
for the sake of economic gain.
If the body is mathematical,
Black bodies have mastered geometric shapes of rectangles and squares
through passages of triangles—obtuse
and scalene—from Africa to the Americas and New England.

They know lines—parallel and perpendicular, red lines,
covenant lines, and lines that lead away from sundown towns.
Black bodies know margins of circles and ellipses where Black trans
bodies represent 80% of all murdered trans Americans
and Black women and girls perform disappearing acts hiding
their Black bodies to the count of almost 75,000. Black bodies
know dying. They know remains of bones and dust bathed
in liquor poured for the brothers and sisters who ain't here.
Black bodies know carrying the sins of a nation on its back.

Black bodies. They know.
They know rising from the ashes
of the thing meant to consume them.
Black bodies know how to be reborn.
They know arms raised in praise and hallelujah
and songs of hymns and spirituals while waiting
for the angel to trouble the water.

Black bodies. They know.
They know rising in rebellion
against the thing meant to subdue them.
Black bodies know liberation.
They know rest as resistance to white supremacy
and capitalism and marching and kneeling in protest.
Black bodies. They know. They know breaking
out from boxes that can no longer contain them.

Gentrification

This city has been dissected and its contents removed
to make space for a Whole Foods, priced-out high-rises, and jogging
folk who call the cops because you look suspicious.
Imagine that! The native suspicious in his own land.

This city has been discovered and claimed
in the same way as the Americas. Your existence in this land null and
void, your humanity discarded in the name of revitalization
and redevelopment, the new colonization and exploitation.

Urban renewal, Negro removal, displacement, subjugation—
what's in a name? The outcome is the same. "No foam, low fat, latte!"
The Starbucks has replaced the barbershop, the neighborhood
bonding spot. You dream, on the metro ride home, of the people of
Saint-Domingue and wish you too could have refused to become a
good servant.

Lines

I.
I cannot swim.
I never learned.
My mother was born in Mississippi in 1941.
She could not swim.
She never learned.
Yet, these waters know me.
They call me by name.
They knew my ancestors,
buried them like treasure.

II.
O' give me—you tired, poor, huddled mass yearning
to breathe—your homes, your community down by the sea.
You tempest-tossed Black and brown bodies, there is no
lit lamp beside the Golden Door you fashioned for thee.

III.
The children are no longer playing.
They have gone.
It is not safe to play here.
The children are no longer children.
They are offerings.
They have been sacrificed for the right to bear arms.

IV.
Skittles, loosies, a counterfeit $20 bill.
Death.
The Aurora Theater, Emanuel African Methodist Episcopal
Church, TOPS Friendly Markets.
Dinner.

Suffer Little Children

(on Marion Palfi's black and white photograph Detroit, Paradise Valley at the Phoenix Museum of Art)

Standing in the entry of the doorway, I plot my path
to climb what remains of our stairs.
Mama said to be careful.
Next time I may not be so lucky.
The splintered wood ripped through my knees
like claws on a blackboard. My salty tears the cleanest
water to touch my lips all year. Truth be told, I'm in
no hurry to go inside. My back turned to a world that has turned
its back on me, I can hear Ms. Fitzgerald singing, *Somebody Nobody*
Loves. Bare feet warmed by the worn fabric strewn about the ground
like a tossed salad. Hands gripping the lapel of some little white girl's
discarded coat. My favorite dress. My only dress.
They call this the Black Bottom.
Where the music is good and the neatly hung refuse
on the line that anchors the door disturbs the sunlight.

The Wind Here

The wind is always best here.
Flags of red, white, and blue
encircling the phallic monument
erected for the first to lead a more perfect
union. The land occupied by the Anacostans,
Piscataway peoples.

The wind is always best here.
It keeps the flags—the star-spangled ones
seen after the bombs burst—fixed in the air.
They flap, they wave, they summon me
to this place.

The wind is always best here.
The chilled marble seats, not kissed
by the warmth of the sun, are nothing more
than markers for graves from genocide.

Yet, each visit I make, I return to it. Perhaps in remembrance,
perhaps in prayer. But always, to ease the guilt, I tell myself
it is because, on a hot summer day, the wind is best here.

Christie Ann Cruise, Ph.D., is an educator, author, and social justice advocate with a passion for empowering Black women and girls to speak their truths boldly and unapologetically. Her passion led her to serve as a mentor with the Reach & Rise Program of the Gateway Region YMCA, an advisory board member for Nia Kuumba Spirituality Center for African and African American Women, treasurer for the Young Ambassadors of the YWCA of Metro St. Louis, and a volunteer for St. Louis Children's Hospital's Raising St. Louis Program. In addition, Dr. Cruise is a member of the Association of Writers & Writing Programs (AWP) and past President of the Board of the International Women's Writing Guild (IWWG).

In 2019, she self-published her first book, *It Don't Hurt Now: My Journey of Self-Love & Self-Acceptance*. Dr. Cruise's poetry, reflections, and self-portrait photography have been published in *Gumbo Magazine, Remington Review, Gallery & Studio Arts Journal, Sunspot Literary Journal, Kitchen Table Quarterly, Black Minds Mag*, the International Women's Writing Guild (IWWG) anthology *Heels Into the Soil: Stories & Poems Resisting the Silence*, and the IWWG Network edition *Our Stories, Ourselves: Narratives from Black Women in Africa and America*. Dr. Cruise has also contributed to blogs for the *Black Mental Wellness Corporation, The Healing Collective Global, Spoken Black Girl*, and *Mahogany by Hallmark*. She was a Peyton Evans Artist in Residence (PEAR) at the Studios of Key West from December 2021 to January 2022. Dr. Cruise is also a 2024 recipient of the Artist Opportunity Grant from the Arizona Commission on the Arts.

Dr. Cruise was born in East St. Louis, Illinois. She received a Bachelor of Science from the University of Illinois at Urbana-Champaign, a Master of Science from Eastern Illinois University, and a Doctor of Philosophy from Bowling Green State University.